DANCING OUT OF THE DARK SIDE

DANCING OUT OF THE DARK SIDE

GLYN HUGHES

Shoestring Press

Typeset and printed by Q3 Print Project Management Ltd,
Loughborough, Leics
(01509) 213456

Published by Shoestring Press
19 Devonshire Avenue, Beeston, Nottingham, NG9 1BS
(0115) 925 1827
www.shoestringpress.co.uk

First published 2005
© Copyright: Glyn Hughes
The moral right of the author has been asserted.
ISBN: 1 904886 21 3

Shoestring Press gratefully acknowledges financial assistance from
Arts Council England

To David Pownall

Thank you for the decades of creative friendship

ACKNOWLEDGEMENTS

Acknowledgements are due to the editors of the following magazines where many of these poems appeared for the first time:

The Scotsman for 'Green'

The London Magazine for 'House' and 'Dolphin and Mermaid'

Tears In The Fence for 'Harriet Scattergood's Bible' and 'I Have Always Been Kept From The River'

Rialto for 'Dancing Out Of The Dark Side'

North for 'Milton's Ghost', 'Himalayan Balsam', 'Donkey and moon', 'Death Of An Unwanted Farmer', 'Pennine Way', 'November 24th Calder Valley' and 'Milton's Ghost'.

Other Poetry for 'Grass Wanderer' and 'Ludd's Mills'

Dream Catcher for 'Stones'

Critical Survey for 'Listening to Larks'

New Statesman for 'Petralona Man'

'The Girl Changed Into A Fawn' appeared in *The Gift*, an anthology published by Stride in aid of the N.H.S. An early version of 'Harriet Scattergood's Bible' was in a *Poetry Book Society Supplement*.

'Mr Lowry' was awarded a prize in the South Warnborough Poetry Competition and broadcast on BBC Radio 4.

'Cleansing', 'Dancing Out Of The Dark Side', 'Death Of An Unwanted Farmer', 'November 24th Calder Valley', 'Bride Stones', and 'Ludd's Mills', formed parts of the BBC Radio 4 programmes that I presented, *Millstone Grit Revisited*. 'Bride Stones' was broadcast in *The Long Causeway*, BBC Radio 4, Jan 10th–14th 2005.

Several poems have been posted on the Hebden Bridge website: http://www.hebdenbridge.co.uk

Thanks also to the friends who have commented upon this volume: especially David Annwyn, Mike Freeman, and Luke Spencer.

CONTENTS

Part 1 North

Part 2 South

Part 3 Home

PART 1

NORTH

GREEN

Once I sat all day in field and lane
to paint the everywhere pouring green.
Slept out in it on month-long wanderings:
green sprinkled with daisies, and the buttercups' candelabras,
and poppies, with their black hearts, and their red,
that seem so bold but are the frailest flowers,
living one day, collapsing in my hands.
Green crushed under the cattle's hooves and tongues,
strained out of the bodies of flies,
and smearing its juice on the farmer's cart.
Green through which birds hurtle and dive.
Green ripening to yellow sinking from the tip
of the corn slowly as the days turn by.
Green associated with mothers:
it was my mother's name.

        I came out of the fields
a green man covered in a cling of seeds
rubbed off the hedgerows. Not quite sane
and awkward in the pubs on summer evenings.
With my smeared paintings,
wanting to be a peasant
as Van Gogh tried to be a priest:
a tunnel, a narrow gate mistaken for a way.

HOUSE

When I came here I had to un-nail the door
and break into its dark. Rain
dripping for years had rotted the floor.
I possessed first a smell of soot and ashes.
I let light in, and, twice, I married,

and left here for Greece
where often I would blink at the light
and long for some, for this dark place,
just as the Greeks did as a matter of fact,
closing shutters and lurking in siestas.

Did I marry that one for her darkness,
did I turn to another for her light?
Then that light too became ashes.
Shadows of marriage haunt the corners
of house, woods, villages and hills.

Today I took our carpets where the cars
of other townsfolk loop around the tip
on this Bank Holiday: a clearance fiesta.
That house I once let light into is soon restored.
Visible, the wood and stone. Bare boards.

I re-discover the long-walled-up fireplaces.
Tonight – a glass of whisky in my hand –
for the first time again I can smell ashes.

MR LOWRY

I would walk from my cottage in the fields –
my paradise of hens and cabbages,
potatoes, marigolds, the common things
of the countryside – knowing the farmers
and happy with my physical well-being.

And at Mottram where the fields ended
I'd come upon Lowry's house from the back:
his mildewed greenhouse,
the littered yard where the painter never looked,
and his housekeeper, Mrs Swindells,
busy among the dustbins.

I'd climb a gate to the bleak main road
of terraces, bungalows and sodium lamps,
and pass the grubby front of The Elms.
Once I paused to listen
to his elegant music: his Donizetti.
The lit, etched glass of his door
held a momentary shadow, and as I fled, I saw
Lowry, like a cadaverous heron
peering – he didn't seem to see me – down the street.

A wealthy miser in a greasy mac who chose
to live in a village he loathed,
he would escape to Manchester where he collected rents.
And even at a bus-stop with the villagers,
by the gritstone church, among the soaked moors
and my paradisial fields, the gentlemanly painter –
first of discarded places, next of empty ones,
and of self-portraits slashed with red
as if with a razor
and seamed with the blue lines of sorrow –
looked wistful and remote
like someone staring through a window.

At Lowry's Retrospective, after he died,
I saw his drawing of my shadow on his door
and his note to it. He was haunted by
a visitor who vanished.
                              Lowry died that way –
aching for visitors, he collapsed as he rushed to the door
for one who did not stay.

DEAD END

Aching to find what is left of old England I stray
off the helltrack of motorways
to a Roman road with a new but apt name –
"Red Route"; now bloodied with accidents,
marked by flowers, grazed posts and stripped tyres.
Prone to seek what still could be sacred –
maybe signed, "Holy Well", or after a saint –
I turn off this too. Once-gracious farmland
put to carcinogens might still show – yes, it does:
an England earlier veiled by the flash of cars.
Around a village of worn stone
gnawing sheep for centuries sculpt
a fabric of herbs and flowers
and bells command in a golden tower
that strikes a blue sky astir with birds.
I park in a dead end and I join
the sublimely forgetful, or so they seem,
ushered to their cosy services.
Within is a sense of voices almost heard,
and shafts of honey light
divide shadows and catch faded pictures
whose solemn icons have lost their meaning,
and only the Devil laughs.

All revives the yearning
that lures us back to a seeming peace –
though spilled blood, cruelty and war
will have marked here more.
What does it give us, the past?
Massage for our sentiments?
Fantasies to match the cast of our minds?
Props for an England of privilege and habit
expressed so softly that we hardly notice
(snobbery masked as humility) until some thrust
out of Ireland, Africa or our appalled North says,
we've had enough, wake from your daze?

Or is it a vast of thinned-out air
where the spirit hovers
and maybe greets with surprise
a new friend caught in a forgotten place;
John Taverner in Boston, say;
a spirit closer than most that are now here,
communicating, out of nowhere, something?

I HAVE ALWAYS BEEN KEPT FROM THE RIVER

1.

I am lounging in a sunny field
with Sunday papers and a litre of wine;
Pendle Hill in the tawny light
of autumn humped like a beast
comfortably at rest in its distance.
With me is Liz whom I've known for a year,
so not a bad time for seventy
(though why should I be more grateful than at twenty?)
enjoying day after day whatever is given
unspooling until the end of our time

like the pouring of the river that we're kept from
with warnings in the extreme misanthropy
that overcomes the English when they own land
or even tenant some.

2.

I have always been kept from the river.
I don't mean the drab bit where the sewage tips,
bridged by ugly pipes and with a tang
where even such as I may fish
(there are no fish) I mean
the thousand delectable miles through England
where every mile a solitary toff
wades or stalks and casts
and for his sake the riverside paths
are year by year fenced further off.

Yet even from here there is a beauty
in that shimmer, warble and glide –
reminder of moments imprinted on my eye,
the twinkle of water manywheres.

3.

When as a child I could not sleep
for thinking of the river through the park
and my footprints marked the dawn-dewed grass
a gamekeeper once
lurked – it must have been for an hour
that he waited by a gap in the fence
through which this poor boy – me –
from the edge of town had entered;

and hammered me with a walking stick
until I outran him, while a rage
as old as England though I did not know it,
as old as Piers Plowman and John Clare's,
took my soul by the hand.

4.

"Ramblers are only of use
when we run out of pheasants to shoot,"
said the Press Officer to the Countryside Alliance
Ms Janet George in '98.

I think of it on this hot day
seeing twenty children kept from the river
and I fancy leading a Children's Crusade
(even one child matters, an absent fisherman doesn't)
down the forbidden bank
into the private shimmer.

5.

Like a river too
is Liz in her cycles pouring
by the orchards of earthly desire
until reaching this pool that we have found for us
this pool of a moment, or years
and whatever desires flow through
I am down there at any rate sometimes,
dabbling in the shallows.

WALKING BY HARDCASTLE CRAGS WITH TED HUGHES

1.

His "first taste of Paradise" he said
of this deep cut in the moor
that ancients walked miles round to avoid
its traps of wet mould and its ghosts;
at its bottom the first river
Ted knew – this peaty tribute
to the black, stained Calder,
churning as usual with light.
I walk here most days and now I re-invent
when I came here with him
on his half-secret returns to the valley
at the time of his huge spawnings of blank verse,
seeking both to remember and to forget;
a drowning in words after Sylvia

he still living truly as himself –
his highest praise for me, for anyone. I recall
his hawk's eye for the world's myths and its mechanics;
and his gate of hair defending his brow –
his cave of arcane secrets
not so much kept, as veiled;
his tribal, atavistic
faith in the divine right of land and of kings.

Of my book dramatising "spiritual genocide"
here in the eighteenth century, he wrote
(with a logic that defeated me at first –
though obvious, it was so unexpected
to define Chartism as a further descent of the soul)

*"That it was also the cradle of the Chartist Movement seems the
next logical step, straight out of Blake's Prophetic books."*

11

2.

I wish I was here with my Dad
and we three could go walking on this autumn day
where the woods are shedding their cascade
in golden shiverings.
To my Dad he'd seem knowing and smart
despite Ted's blackened nails and farmer's hands.
My Dad was a Union man, apologetic and bold
at once, as they were in those days.
I hear his flat-vowelled, Manchist'r voice
against Ted's Viking gutterals.

"Ted, it was for them chances that you had
of the Grammar School and Cambridge
while we were only learned to do what's right,
that we all fought hard for it."

3.

An age separated him from Ted's bold thought:
the mutual ecstasy of predator and prey,
hunter and hunted – Ted and Sylvia –
Nazi and Jew.
This would have been anathema to my Dad,
or so he'd say
yet also would leave him wondering, and maybe excited:
was it true?

They talk – though most of what goes beyond
sexual clinchings is left out,
as usual with men. Their sadness
pulls at their feet like the mould,
in that last age when the guilt
of men was more easily exorcised.
Ted throws his glance over all the beauty and says:

*"We know about as much of what's truly going on as someone
who, looking out to sea, catches sight of a fin."*

12

4.

Light is merrying from a low, cool sun
on tree tops in a line-dance of light.
Unveiled branches reach out of their leaf-fall
in a damp silence and stillness.
It is as if I'm the only creature in the world.
The air has a faint bite promising frost,
but is still earth scented.

How often have I walked here, wanting
to tire my thoughts, or find them explained
through an insight out of Nature that never comes;
out of a beauty that seems to have meaning
but is only an abstraction
from what cares nothing for us; yet still hoping
for some clearance of the head and heart
so that one can see and feel,
say, that bush there flaming in autumn colour.

At least in this, two, three can be one.

FIDDLE WOOD

1.

At last I am able to love again
my wood – the rivertorn cleft,
its lodges, goits and old mill-workings:
grooves carved in stone by wheels of harder stone
and water wrung out
through every drain and spout.
The wood outside my window that for thirty years
I've loved as a mistress –
with lapses of fidelity.

Can a wood have a soul?
In the valley's whirlpool of air,
in the swirl of anxious ghosts,
are footsteps, presences
of the long, old path from Humber to Morecambe Bay.

2.

I have seen on many summers' days
huge, imagined faces
lean out of the wood:
the bulbous, bushy-browed, green
monsters projected by medieval life
out of what they feared: strangers coming,
villainous or merely hungry
but always dangerous

where mill-girls going to work in the morning dark
feared ghosts and linked their arms.

ROCK ROSE
A poem inscribed in a Pennine graveyard,
Mill Bank, West Yorkshire.

Love and remember the many before us,
their hearts no better sealed than ours,
Chartists, Methodists, the fellow and sister yearners,
ill-treated in mills but not broken,
their ghosts for ever drifting the Sublime.
Hammer and chisel, ledger and pen,
cradle and loom are rested,
hewn stone is overgrown or sweetened
and sacredness of field and wood restored.
Happiness is frail when entrusted to human hands
and leaves only shadows.
Here pray that upon the stones of fear or hate
may grow the flowers of loving,
the rock rose.

LUDD'S MILLS

Ludd was their King Arthur,
their proletarian sun-god,
a strider of and glow upon the hills
whose magic would bring
health to their children and straight bones
and quiet hours in which to study.

It didn't happen
though over Ludd's scarred land
the occupier's pastoral dream
survives with streams of silver-
leafed woodlands are revived
and the hillsides ribbed again with freshened deans.

DANCING OUT OF THE DARK SIDE

Everyone who lives here shuns the dark sides
of valleys where the sun never shines,
where only the poor go
for a life stunted by hopelessness.

There they lose the rhythm of sun-dwellers
and turn into stone,
staring across to where the sun is,
too dazzled to see the life that is there.

I, the partner without melody or dance
and exhausted by my dark side stare
at the side that has the sun from her face
and in the toss of her hair.

FOXES

Wind and rain died and dark days fled,
silence of ice and clear skies came
with birds and animals, tamed by hunger,
wheeling, begging, hunting.

　　　　　One night a fox
came out of its night world.
Pregnant with its otherness
it was caught in the lights of my old Rover.
We saw each other and were changed.

How vividly I also remember
fox and mate tracking over the moonlit snow.
There'd be cubs soon. In autumn I'd heard
the dark valley becoming
a black well filled with howls,
the noise of their fucking.

They had come for our poultry carcasses.
Two that – flowing like moonlit mercury
on either side of the field below –
when regarding each other, echoed our own glances;
each an other-world messenger for the other
running on the bottom of our sleep.

MILTON'S GHOST

I am in the pub taproom where Milton did his ironing
in the quiet hours, but mostly Mrs Buckley's
and hung it on a "maiden" by the fire
that he had lit and polished the brasses.
Milton Appleyard is who I mean.
A tough and self-contained ex-farmer
fallen on bad, or was it good times,
he hand-washed and ironed
the undies of his dumpy odalisque
and served her in her hidden place
(their teeth in mild bleach by the bed, fancy that)
then fetched beer in a jug
where Buckley dared not enter and Mrs didn't
among starched underwear and blouses.
He swept it, scrubbed it, ruled it,
choosing never to leave his bed and board
except to bring warm eggs in from the grass
or hang out washing above the roaming hens.

I catch it fortunately in its near-silence
and warmth of embers trapped from last night.
An hour like those that made their honeymoon;
that time when calls of poultry, curlews, larks
and Buckley's grumbles invaded their window.
One pint of beer in the early evening
and I could almost live here again –
just as I almost did in the past,
like Milton with "my feet under the table",
as welcome as any for my wit and my money.
The moor outside and this taproom-kitchen –
"the poor man's study", as one dialect poet wrote –
is still the same; a stone floor, and a flagged *ceiling,*
and through the peephole window a damp green light
where crows tossed in the breaths
of thermals over the wood are dancing
but are really just blown on threads of air.

19

They have nests to steady them somewhere
and I, a pint of Lees' dark bitter in my hand,
hold a dim thought of not being chucked out at eleven,
of not being chucked out ever – Milton's ghost.

GRASS WANDERER

He smells of cows.
I sniff it across ten acres of this grass
about which he knows all there is
to be known by tasting and looking:

how it silvers the fields
with its seeds and in the heat grows
heavy-headed and tired like himself
and stoops to its rest.

Sucking from a stalk
the poison sprayed on roadsides he seems
sleepy when he walks. He seems
as natural as a cow-flop to this earth.

He is looking sideways at you, but he stays
in the fields' custody, like the cows.

DEATH OF AN UNWANTED FARMER

1.

Down in the village the in-comers
drive assault-craft and jungle-invaders.
Well, they're just motorcars, really.
The rest is their dream.
Polished off-roaders
ready for school-runs through the Spring showers
and other hazards of cottage life.

Too wide for our lanes, they shunt and quarrel,
especially with Harry in his Ford –
carrier of sheep, straw bales,
and a compost of beer-cans, fag-ash and *The Sunday Sport.*

2.

Harry on his moor hates all the strangers
though most of what he knows is their bullying cars
and their maddening lightheartedness
that he calls, 'only playing at it,'
which is part of their love of his enemy, the Pennine moor.
He hates all walkers and their undisciplined dogs.
He barbed-wires the footpaths, and would landmine them if he
                                                        could.

But did he ever contemplate,
as they do, the light's dance over the moor,
the lapwing's down-sky plunge of rapture,
or the river of delight that was, before he fouled it,
the stream by his door?

Their frisson of space collapses into what he's despised:
soured land, ugly erosions,
and old quarries filled with rubbish –
Harry's spiritual, unshared home.
'Hikers and horsey folk this way,' reads the daub
on his barn wall – pointing into his midden.

3.

Backslider, sprung from a line of chapel-attenders,
at night he drinks in *The Headless Woman*.
(Much the best kind of woman, he says.)

'It's same as a say!
With the lefties, poufters and bossy women
that have taken over the teevee and the wireless ...
what about men of my age what have fought ...'

Afterwards he indulges what he believes are illegal pleasures –
in his farm's filth listening on short-wave radio
to taxi-drivers, ambulances, fire and police calls,
with no speech of his own but a
growl like stones down a scree
rolling through silence
into darkness ...

PICKLES FARM

In at the gate then, after a hesitation
from forboding, dismissed as irrational.
It hangs well, the gate, and is wide enough for cattle
though I saw none.
Comforting that there are no improvements
and paintwork's that old-fashioned crimson
loved by farmers, kept up every year.
In the yard's a wringer
for wet clothes, and it's used and clean.
Stretched across the yard, a washing line
has broad-beamed trousers hanging from it.
They're hardly "washed", in modern terms,
yet I can be sure (I think) some woman's done it.
The yard is messy, in a way
vanished from the hill-farms of today.
(The neighbours are all commuters.)
But where are the beasts? Where is the *life?*
I open a barn door. It's empty
yet stock's not kept out now, it's winter.
Above a scrubbed bench and a porcelain sink
is a row, fifteen or so I think, of shining knives.
Cross the yard, next. Knock at the house door and there comes
a flushed man, dazed as if he's been watching television,
at any rate he's sunk into
a life that's not to do with here, today.

It is many years ago –
a time when bees and flies made up the hum
that now a motorway five miles off melts into –
that often I would tumble from the moor
and come in through a gate like this, find such a man,
through patient weeks make friends,
sensing his self-containment as a charm
such as only he might have,
he so organic with what I loved most then.
Such farmers as he – history's residues
living in a world as it once was –
do they simplify complexities
or tighten them in knots of prejudice?

Maybe he's said all he wants to say
as you see old folks in public houses
gone there to be with others yet saying nothing.
He doesn't want me inside, I can see that.
He starts a kind of laughing,
not in a way I like, but lets me in.

People lead their real lives in secret, said Chekhov;
that there's a mystery here's as palpable
as say the hot stove, or a smell of dog,
or jam on the towel that looks maybe
like lipstick that a woman has smeared.
(I remember those capacious trousers.)
The jam, I notice now, is on everything...

I fled with nothing to say.
It was as if the body that was killed in there was mine;
my old self.
        So out to the unmusical, moorland birds
that only scream and cry across the twilight.
Under the down-blown chimney-smoke
a crow shuffles and an early owl
squats on a stump – stumped,
not wise enough to know the day from night
while over the moor the stars come out
throbbing electric, red to blue.

PASTORAL

This was the crowd with which we lived,
all the company I needed, all our profit
staring in at the window. I too was outside it.
Yelling and prodding, I stood at the gate,
knowing that these slow transmitters of birth
cannot be harried yet hurrying them,
my wellingtons stuck in muddy earth;
a slave to that yet a prince among cattle.

I watch them roll from field to barn
and toil at their chewing,
all their restlessness in their tongues
otherwise placid though the fear
constant in the moons of their sad eyes
quickens when a dog starts or a truck arrives.

                    I stood with my tribe
as a wild animal by a house where lamps are lit
among sounds of humans and their scent;
I not happier, yet more able,
at least more ready to bolt – though in there was my home.

When their limbs stiffened in their Winter stalls
I saw them through it, I shovelled out
sweet-smelling excrement. An expert shoveller,
I'd learned to scoop it with a swift
lift after a slow glide – just so –
and barrow the steaming load outside.

The growing midden was my calendar
until on a chosen Spring day, through
a thousand rays of lark song
I slapped and drove, chivvying life back
into the stately queens of the pasture.

We held a wakes when the emptied fields
urged us to quicken ourselves to another life
and guiltily celebrate:
"Thank God I'm not a beast."

Their dribbling rumps ascending the ramp to the cart,
their lowing before execution,
then silence in the deserted fields and heart.

NOVEMBER 24TH, CALDER VALLEY

West Yorkshire light today is as clear as Arles,
the hills are cobalt blue and
although it is cold in the wind
sun in the valley brings a smell of pines.

He steps from the slum of his rusting Ford
leaving his music playing.
In baseball cap and cement-clogged trainers
he is more rabbit than 'cowboy' of the building trade
burrowing, wandering, and officially unemployed.
He's moved in next door to live alone.

How do you like it here? I ask.
He stares at the emptiness he's put up with for a week –
trees fan their bright blades through the wood in the light –
then tightens on an important question.

'It's alright now I've a stereo in the car.'

PENNINE WAY

1.

For bedside reading, a Gideon bible
and Charlotte Bronte's *Book of Jokes.*
Younger hikers,
wet through, irrepressible, drunk,
are at it in the barn.

I face the hush of breakfast:
a greasy devouring, restored to sacrament
or at least to awe; to silence,
or a whisper:
"The flood were 'orrendous.
It buggered the Sky,
we couldn't get no football."

Beyond the window and a
swinging sock of nuts
are moors and an ancient wood
gashed with new, white falls of water.

The waxproofed horsewomen are clopping by.
The enviable fuckers troop out of the barn.
A rag of cerulean blue
breaks the sky.

2.

Sunrise and the frosted hill
becomes an iridescent pearl,
frost-grained all the afternoon
warmed briefly into ochre lights –
colour of fields that yesterday we knew.
Then a faint warm sweetness scents the air;
odour of grass that feels the sun.
Frost lasts in shadows cloudily
ribboned with black water.

STONES

1.

Above many of the towns are
touchstones to another state of being
beneath the stars, or in the sun
with heather blooming
but few look up and fewer climb
out of Cough Valley or Carcinogen Clough.

Though when trying to forge one truth –
to integrate the wandering spirit –
this is the place to be; where anchoring the skies
has hardly marked them and they bear
names of myths and archetypes,
Ludd's, or Saint Bridie's stones.

2.

Leave an indoor life caught on hooks
and the phone that threatens to ring.
Find self: a spring bubbling, clearing
its way through frozen water.

Or is 'self' an old, paved way
for sturdy packhorses, lying
in a straight line over the hills,
still, though under the grass?

BRIDE STONES

Warm in the valleys – but June up there
was wild and cold as a Shetland winter,
at least it felt like it,
and a wind brewed gods knew where
chiseled those Ice Age cuttings.

The moor was in its flowering –
cotton-grass in drifts of white
glazes lighter than the sky;
snipe and curlew weaving
through warps of rain.

In an evening's murmur of settling birds
on a moor that still accumulates probes –
radio masts and telescopes –
I find stone antennae,
a touching, through rain, of the awakening stars.

LISTENING TO LARKS

Following rain on a hot soil hardened
without moisture came the Promethean
forging of earth, fire and water into Spring.
This year all nature is restored
and more awake than ever before
with the flowers of a now dulled childhood.
And the larks,
those sound-stars pulsing against the blue,
telling me that the preciousness of each day
justifies this will and joy.

OLD MAN

Until the end of sunset the chestnut tree
clutched a ray of light to its heart

and the old man always sat under it, as if he felt
that holding a light within the surrounding dark
showed the proper way to depart.

PART 2

SOUTH

SOUTH

Dordogne and Lot and Provence and the Pyrenees
are where this strayed Northerner wanders
trying to remember what he is looking for;
one of three million in a day
leaping on their fellow travellers' tails,
car heat and sun melting the tarmac.

As in all journeys he travels two in one.
One is of payage, rest-stops and old towns.
(Their squares where heretics were burned now offer cool hotels).
The other is in his head,
not knowing how to express himself nor what to express
until he arrives where Calvin never trod
where red wine colours faces and flushes the earth.

Winter has peeled back and oven heat
dancing among flowers melts those senses
that served him in the North
until possessed by new thoughts, as the South
releases its spirits of butterflies, of flowers.

PETRALONA MAN

(Antedating Cro-Magnon Man, he was discovered in a cave in northern
Greece, in sight of Mount Olympus.)

Ghost, messenger from the horizon
of history, peering, frightened, he came in
from the ice with other beasts –
this animal-man whose skull they've found
among the stalagmites in the dark;
the floor thick with bones and droppings,
and all as dark as his low skull, flickering
with questions; at his side an accidental fire that he kept alive
thousands of years by tugging logs to it.

After how long was it before his descendants
beyond animal tenderness discovered love
and did not discard their mother's bones
but thought of graves and memorials?
Demeter and Aphrodite were born in cave-dreams –
their statues erected in dark temples
stained with the mess and blood of sacrifice:
a memory of wombs and caves.

The ice melted, earth turned green and bright.
As frightened as he'd been to enter, he came out
and saw across sea and plain
this same view of Mount Olympus,
its vast sunlit saddle a seat of the gods.

CARPE DIEM

1.

Dining outdoors on roast lamb, honey and rosemary:
"Carpe diem," I said, while sipping Chablis
as the world seemed rushing into World War Three.

2.

Once, rubbing in my hands a perfumed tinder
of origano on a Greek hillside,
and taking with a glass of water
at a plastic table outside a taverna
a joy translucent and transcendent,
I turned to see the names
inscribed after a massacre.

There was a small museum, bright with sun;
hens, goats, wandering;
artifacts of pottery, weaving, stone
where sunlight and sea's erosion merely honed
the *carpe diem* of an art
carved in the pauses of tribal wars,
despite the wanton gods.

Sparta and Athens; Hitler and us.
The mind can tell itself:
keep this or that in its cave,
your dark thoughts will be there when you want them,
but not joy, always.
For now, to sit dappled in the shade
of a blossoming tree is to be graced and blessed.

WATERCOLOURS

1. At Vouliagmeni

Jellyfish like half-transparent roses
flower a few hours before
the sleek sea turns to clean itself
and a wild sheet of light breaks up on the shore.

Oily sheets of plastic float.
A gull's white flashes like a star –
one moment transparent and the next dark,
lunging on the beat of its wings.

2. Poppies

Drop by drop
the poppies' red
splashes on the stony fields
so brightly that it scalds my eyes.

O the glare of flowers
lighting up scorched olive groves
where the spiders scatter
like spit upon a stove!

The hot earth smells
like food brought from the oven.
Scattered with chaff and dried weeds,
it glows like an icon.

3. Spring

The Greeks still call it *orgasmos physos*:
'nature's orgasm'
at its climax in these waves of flowers,
beginning in Africa,
leaping across the islands, Crete and Paros.

Following the first timid events – crocus, saxifrage;
white daisies that turn to the light like faces
of a theatre crowd following the action – spring was flung
from over the sea horizon, south.

Wave after wave came. I could not work,
but every day had to go out and look
and worship what had come
to amaze us before it passed on
in spasms, northwards.

4. Donkey and moon

A donkey roars and grazes
the earth's fierce cover: thorns
that put out flowers on sides not burned by the sea.

The moon is a pearl surrounded by
a ring of blue clear as a baby's eye

and two circles of rainbow
over mountains of thorn and marble
at sunset tarted in amazing pink.

5. Athens

In streets named after Sophocles,
Aristotle, Pericles,
the glittering cars pour like a torrent
of sweat beads from a body;
circle the ancient rocks,
Acropolis, Lycavittos,
then rush off to the sea to bathe
as if panic stricken.

Air stinks of sun oil
and sun is the stroke of hot iron on the head
in the wavering, half visible
river of petrol fume.

6. The Acropolis

From the air, a white speck floating
in a moat of pollution,
nicotine brown, ringing the horizon,
is the Athens Acropolis.
White, dry, gleaming like salt,
it is bleached of its red ochre,
its atmosphere of the womb
and its slaughterhouse blood.

7. An abandoned monastery, Siphnos

Now a numinous image flakes
from a broken wall
where the peasant and his mule
plough with crooked sticks
around forgotten runics
with a soft footfall.

THEATRE

Years ago I visited the places,
or some of them, that teach us:
art is for healing. Epidavros was one:
a theatre scooped out of the grass
that was dried to gold and weighted with light
and which I likened to a child's drawing of the sun.
There my friend, Nicos Papaconstantinos,
played the messenger in *Antigone*.
For days we discussed those absolutes of fate
that steer us through the tides of thought and will.

Today my grandson potters on the lawn
following his moment's need,
doing what seems to him invented.
Yet I marvel at how I am in him
and can guess what he might do tomorrow.
In deeds that seem willed he uses my eyes.
It was my grandchild stole my fear of death,
Antigone's lesson, and now, though I don't want to, I
can fly.

LEMON JUICE

The stores and cafés were closed for the winter.
The mansions were shut on the peninsula,
the Lebanese and Ethiopean
maids were their only visitors
arriving at dawn from Athens to meet the sun,
the winter flowers and the vast shimmer that
brought black-sailed Theseus over the sea.

And in the garden of our flat –
a holiday home let for the winter –
was the lemon tree I raided for its hoard
to make *lemonada* beneath an olive tree
in a January more bright than an English summer.

In a different marriage I show how to do it –
the table-fork moved like a pendulum
across each cheek sliced from a lemon,
and the juice trailed over salad for its piquancy

leaving on my hands
a final, cleansing sting of bitterness.

PART 3

HOME

DOLPHIN AND MERMAID

1.

I have seen dolphins. They are shyness and delight
embodied and a school of them share their joy
skipping out of the sea, disappearing
at the first throb of ships' motors.

One bucks and rides through my sweetheart's dreams.
Slippery in the sun, he's her grey animus,
animal but part-fish and so shy
that each morning he plunges back into her unconscious

leaving his trail across the day
as at twilight the water birds
and rising fish leave their wakes
in silver scars like comets across lakes.

2.

And I have seen mermaids. Especially one
carved in the Saxon church at Nately Scures:
a sea-messenger as truly mine as if I had dreamed her.
For this church is a closed other-world like a dream –

the weight of walls, slit windows, the curved apse,
scarred statues, and wedges of cream light
cutting the womb-dark. A thousand years
so stirs the ghosts, I dare not close the doors.

A sailor (from this landlocked place)
was drawn through coils of this mermaid's lust.
What second self had now discovered him
when at sea – his conscious with unconscious linked?

Returning to marry his old sweetheart,
it was his mermaid awaited him at the church.
Musicians and guests stopped at the sight
as she swept him down the rivers to where he
would remain in bondage to the sea.

47

3.

It's summer, the trees swell with green, I'm overwhelmed
and restless with my mermaid self, the dolphin's sister.
I feel like warm moist sleepy earth,
the soil of Edens longed and lusted for:
religion's memories; explorers' desires.

Though I've learned that there's no Eden but ourselves,
male and female taking part. Then suddenly
its summer gardens are spread out in your heart.

PASSING OUT

Once I was a boy who knew
there was no Paradise but this:
days and nights under the sky with a friend
known long enough to be quiet
when lit by our epiphanies.
Moonrise startling a perfumed valley.
Waking in a thick of bird-call.
I was possessed by glowings.

Now age brings its ironic slant
On my visit to the doctors.
Mocking all the sex I've ever enjoyed,
beautiful nurses dive
rubber-gloved into my orifices
merely to keep alive
one deprived of the air
of so many friendships, so much love.

Thus vacuum-packed for dying
on an orthopaedic bench I stare
upwards into the eyes
of my captors' cloudy masks and their eyes
(one is blue, the other of infinite sands)
with my despicable melting eyes of a trapped hare.

WITCH HUNT

1.

I wonder if dreams are waiting to be entered
like countries we are flying to?
Barring crash or hijack there is no escape,
the pilot is out of reach and imperturbable
and there's no landing strip until we arrive.
The figures in those landscapes, waiting.

Whenever dreams show me that my life is stale
it is this woman who conveys it
at Customs or on a rock by the sea.
Hiding her face and crouched in mourning
she turns each dream into the same place.

I never feel sorry for her in dreams,
only when awake. I panic then.
Is she my dead mother's soul? Or a past wife
I've not seen for years but who might now look like that?

Or is she a warning not to let my life be spent
becoming the bruised and ravaged wreck
of a voyage with a bad anima?
With that perversity holding the world in thrall?

Creator of madness, breaker of friends,
inspirer of presidents to bad deeds
and their followers with hubris
she devastates old nations
and leaves the desert of her purpose.

2.

Last night I was in a place where Nebuchadnezzar
might have crawled to eat grass.
There she was an imbecile old crone
condemned to the starved fate
of guarding the dusty hoard of my words
in a dark abandoned farmhouse precariously
balanced above the bright
prospect of Vanity Fair whirled below.
A dark priest took me there.

3.

Sometimes she is too bright to look upon.
She burns my eyes like the sun. At others too dark,
and so like Death that we do not talk of her.
Formless herself, I've imagined her shape
in others and called it "love",
consuming them in that vanity.

Someday I'll leave my house,
perhaps distracted, not myself,
as often when shopping or in traffic
and from the car in front
she'll raise her chin and unscarf her terrible face.

AN ABORTION

In Richmond the forsythia
blazed under showers of light
as someone worked with a plunger
on my girl-friend of the time
to suck out the bloody slime.
For the sake of my own life I adjusted
and headed for Richmond Hill
and thirty years of forgetting,
snared in blind will.
It was just legal then –
it still feels a crime
as I sit on a bench with other old men
and with thirty years of our ghost child,
twisting it into rhyme.

HIMALAYAN BALSAM

You have trod the path between head and heart
and now you have finished your letter: this cage
of venom, or of a new life.
You cannot judge.

Having written it –
with a sharpened knife when you remember how angry you are,
with feathers when you thought who would receive it;
with calculated desire
to close the door yet leave it open
as you think what love once meant

go down the street, slow as a funeral.
Then walk until you forget
that you have posted love's *coup de grace*.
Take down the icons that lost their meaning;
the photos with the endearing words.

You see a flower that knows in its cells about this.
It is beautiful but its scent is caustic as acid.
The Himalayan Balsam also explodes and dies
but that is not the end at all
for the root lies
stronger for sacrifice of leaf and flower.

THE GIRL CHANGED INTO A FAWN

for an autistic child

1.

Her mother lies until midday,
her curtains pinned
to shut out the light
of which she only knows
because their edges show a brighter grey.
She lies by noise imprisoned:
her daughter, dancing above
the ceiling's an iron press
upon her. She lies
scared of her,
that she may not be good.

2.

Outside her room, the wood
has a beauty you
"might die to see and hear." Its moods
are anxious in winds,
stately in summer or in snow
and dainty when rippled by snakes of rain.
Tread softly if you go
for you might stir
among the fallen, flooded boughs,
a sipping deer.

3.

When her lover comes, she peers
from her bed at him, dazed
with wonder if he'll be able to stand it.
'Don't speak to her at all,' she says. *'Don't even try it.'*
And ... *'What if she turns out to be evil ...wicked?'*

Mothers and daughters –
you'd never guess how they can fester.
The poison from all plants and creatures
that are locked in shades and holes!

4.

Can a wood have a soul?
This one has anxious ghosts,
swirling presences

where her child dances
alone upon the pivot of her joy
and of her danger.

5.

Long-legged, fleet and weird,
feral and hunted
on her edge of alarm,
sometimes she runs away.

I could imagine her changed into a fawn,
her life spent with that herd
of sister souls, become the soul of the wood,
to keep on running, like breezes, like water.

Instead, this mother and daughter
try to gather the logic of a day
that has no logic;
is made of a child's light-footed
fawn-like impulse in house and wood;
she who skips and darts so beautifully
when she is dancing.

HARRIET SCATTERGOOD'S BIBLE

1.

They had beautiful names:
Harriet Scattergood who married William Green
for service in country houses and preferred it
to their son's shovelling potash for ICI –
a lifetime finished with his throat
burned out to halt a cancer.

No memories. No pictures. No letters.
No legacy except a Bible inscribed
*To Harriet Scattergood with Mrs Hall
1870* in which she wrote
her record of births and marriages.

Her firm small hand grows large and quavering.
*My darling husband died
1909* and in that new handwriting
the record plunges on, to me.

2.

Her mistress went to Surrey. They went, too.
Then Cheshire. I was born there,
in a smashed-up landscape that she loathed.
A "salt works" that scorched a park with chemicals;
a pungent landscape that flares and screams,
brown like the pages of my grandmother's Bible
which an uncle without a voicebox left to me.
A speechless uncle who showed me wild violets –
a scarf round his throat.

What had he said, once? Hints for saving candles,
tips for polishing shoes and grates,
while a poisonous anguish crept through his features –
I witnessed it – before
the history, gargling useless in his throat,
revolted and had to be burned out.
He pretended he wasn't in pain. And pointed.

56

JUST THIS

Just this. My grandson and I
(he's three) go down to the brook
to warm tinned beans on a camper's fire.
So still an autumn day,
each ribbon of brook song is disentangled.
Broken summer is fallen in harebells' blue.
Hogwood and meadowsweet arch over his sky.

Yet something for which there are no words has entered in
and of which one day we might speak
("Thomas, do you remember when?")
late at night around a different fire.
Will ever again tinned beans, and stones thrown into a stream,
be the happiest time of life –
except when he too is a father, then a grandfather?

THE CENTIPEDE

In one brilliant moment there is your own soul's breath
searing in baby flesh
and dipping into curious things,
puddles and leaves.

A small hand is gripping your finger,
pulling you into the garden,
where the blossom he taps to see the snowy flutter
is that entranced moment that lasts beyond life
and might have come before it: an infinite
moment that waited for its entrance here.

Dig – dig here. He shows you a centipede –
the vital lightening, a single flame
of gold he's never seen before.

And neither, you realise, have you.
What the something is that fills your nothingness
is not his showing you how to dig,
but how to love.